HILLSIDE PUBLIC LIBRARY

3 1992 00210 0205

MAR 0 2 2016

W9-ATF-546

HILLSIDE PUBLIC LIBRARY
405 N. HILLSIDE AVENUE
HILLSIDE, IL 60162
708-449-7510

VIETNAM

by Max Winter

Hillside Public Library

The Child's World

Published by The Child's World®
1980 Lookout Drive • Mankato, MN 56003-1705
800-599-READ • www.childsworld.com

Acknowledgments
The Child's World®: Mary Berendes, Publishing Director
Red Line Editorial: Editorial direction
The Design Lab: Design
Amnet: Production

Design element: Shutterstock Images; Asaf Eliason/
Shutterstock Images
Photographs ©: Hoang Cong Thanh/Shutterstock Images,
cover (right), 19; Shutterstock Images, cover (left, center top),
cover (left center), cover (left bottom), 1 (top), 1 (bottom, top
left), 1 (bottom right), 16 (top left), 16 (right), 21, 24, 25;
Asaf Eliason/Shutterstock Images, cover (left, center bottom),
1 (bottom, bottom left), 16 (bottom left); iStockphoto, 5,
8, 12, 13, 15, 20, 27, 30; Jimmy Tran/Shutterstock
Images, 6–7, 28; Van Thanh Chuong/Shutterstock Images,
10; Hoang Tran/Shutterstock Images, 11; Lauren Ava/
Shutterstock Images, 14; Kenny Thai/Shutterstock Images,
22; Thanh Nghi/Shutterstock Images, 26

Copyright © 2016 by The Child's World®
All rights reserved. No part of this book may be
reproduced or utilized in any form or by any means
without written permission from the publisher.

ISBN 9781634070607
LCCN 2014959733

Printed in the United States of America
Mankato, MN
July, 2015
PA02268

ABOUT THE AUTHOR

Max Winter has written and edited many books about social studies and science for young readers. The subjects of these books have ranged from the Statue of Liberty to building one's own radio.

VIỆT NAM

ONE WORLD • MANY COUNTRIES

TABLE OF CONTENTS

ARCTIC
OCEAN

ATLANTIC
OCEAN

PACIFIC
OCEAN

PACIFIC
OCEAN

VIETNAM

INDIAN
OCEAN

SCALE
0   1000 Miles
0   1000 KM

N
W   E
S

SOUTHERN
OCEAN

VIETNAM

Vietnam is shaped
like the letter S.
It covers 127,881
square miles
(331,210 sq km).
This makes it just
a little larger than
the state of New
Mexico.

FUN FACT

ONE WORLD . MANY COUNTRIES

VIETNAM

CHAPTER 1

WELCOME TO VIETNAM!

In southern Vietnam, flat land stretches for miles. Some areas are covered with water. In other areas, tall grasses sway in the wind. People in boats move slowly down a river. Some are fishing. Others are harvesting plants. Some are having boat races! This is the Mekong **Delta**.

The Mekong Delta was made by the Mekong River. The delta formed where the river flows into the ocean. The delta's flat land and the river's water make good farmland. Rice,

Girls from the Mekong Delta ride down the river in a boat.

sugarcane, and fruit trees grow well there. Workers spend all day in the sun, caring for their crops.

Animals live in the Mekong Delta, too. Water buffalo live in the swamps and forests. People ride them like horses. Catfish swim in the darker parts of the water. Sting rays slither across the river bottom. Dolphins splash and play in the water.

These wild animals and rich land belong to Vietnam. It is small country in Asia. It has a large population for a country of its size. Parts of Vietnam are quiet and beautiful. Other parts are packed with people.

Vietnam's industries are known all over the world. The rice grown in Vietnam is eaten in many countries. Vietnam is perhaps best known for its great beauty. Its mountains, lakes, swamps, forests, and rivers are very beautiful. They make up the exciting, ancient land of Vietnam.

Boys ride water buffalo in wet rice fields.

CHAPTER 2

THE LAND

Mountains rise in northern Vietnam.

Vietnam is in Southeast Asia. China lies to the north of Vietnam. Laos and Cambodia are to its west. Eastern Vietnam borders three bodies of water. They are the Gulf of Tonkin, the South China Sea, and the Gulf of Thailand.

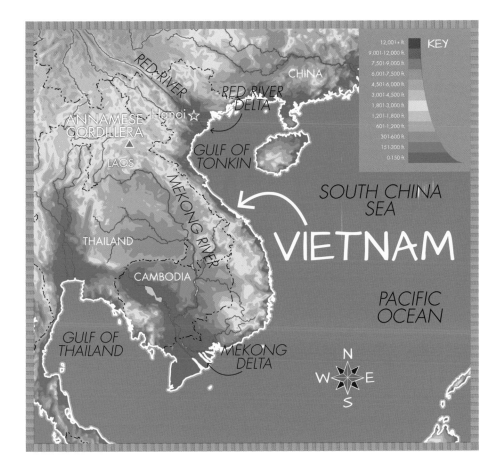

Mountain peaks soar above many parts of Vietnam. The largest mountain range is the Annamese Cordillera. It runs across the country, from west to east. It forms the border between Vietnam and Laos.

Rivers and streams that flow down the west side of the Annamese drain into the Mekong River. It is in southern Vietnam. The river flows for 2,700 miles (4,345 km). It runs through several countries. Then it drains into the South China Sea.

— The Red River

The Red River flows through northern Vietnam. It picks up silt along the way. The silt is deposited along the delta. So much silt arrives there that the delta is growing 328 feet (100 m) each year. The Red River flows into the Gulf of Tonkin.

The Mekong River and the Red River both have deltas and plains. These two areas have rich soil. They are good for farming. Farming is an important part of Vietnam's **economy**. It provides jobs for more than half of Vietnam's people.

Many Vietnamese farmers grow rice. It is Vietnam's most important crop. Rice is grown in fields called paddies. The paddies have 2 to 4 inches (5 to 10 cm) of standing water. The rice grows well in the wet conditions. Much of Vietnam's rice is **exported** to other countries.

In addition to farmland, Vietnam has other natural resources. The land is rich in coal. It is the most important mineral mined in Vietnam. The coal is most often used to generate electricity. The chemicals found in coal can be used to make plastics, dyes, and other goods.

Vietnam's climate is generally warm. In the winter, temperatures are around 60 degrees Fahrenheit (16°C). It is

A farmer tends to rice growing in a paddy in Chau Doc, Vietnam.

often quite windy. In the summer the temperatures average 80 degrees Fahrenheit (27°C). Heavy rains fall often in the summer. Sometimes strong storms called typhoons hit. They start in the ocean. Then they move to land, where they may destroy buildings and houses.

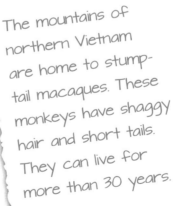

The mountains of northern Vietnam are home to stump-tail macaques. These monkeys have shaggy hair and short tails. They can live for more than 30 years.

FUN FACT · ONE WORLD · MANY COUNTRIES

VIET NAM

CHAPTER 3

GOVERNMENT AND CITIES

Vietnam's official name is the Socialist Republic of Vietnam. It is made up of 58 provinces. They are similar to states. Provinces are led by local governments. Vietnam also has five municipalities. They do not have local leaders. The national government makes all the decisions for them.

The People's Committee Building in Ho Chi Minh City was built by the French in 1909. It was originally a hotel. Today, it is an office building for local leaders.

Citizens vote for lawmakers who serve in the National Assembly. It meets three times each year. Members of the assembly select Vietnam's president. The president represents Vietnam when meeting with leaders from other countries. The president is also in charge of Vietnam's military.

Another important job of the president is selecting the prime minister. Once the president has selected someone, the National Assembly votes. If approved, this person becomes the prime minister. The prime minister runs the government.

Hanoi's Old Quarter is a section of the city that has had shops since the 13th century. The street names in the Old Quarter reflect the goods sold there. There is Hang Gai (Silk Street), Hang Tre (Bamboo Street), Hang Bac (Silver Street), and Hang Huong (Incense Street).

FUN FACT · ONE WORLD MANY COUNTRIES · VIETNAM

Motorbikes are a quick way to get from place to place in Ho Chi Minh City.

The national government meets in Hanoi. It is the capital of Vietnam and the country's second-largest city. Hanoi is in northern Vietnam, along the Red River.

Hanoi is an important center of business. Factories there make goods such as motors, generators, and fabric. Farmers near Hanoi grow rice, fruit, and vegetables. Many of these foods are exported to other countries.

South of Hanoi is Ho Chi Minh City. It is the largest city in Vietnam. About 6.4 million people live there. It is a colorful city that is full of energy. Motorbikes zoom down streets. They serve as taxis, taking riders to the city's many shops and restaurants. Delicious smells rise from food stalls lining the streets.

Like Hanoi, Ho Chi Minh City is an important center of business. Factories there produce goods such as food, soap, bicycles, fabric, glass, and paper. Many of these goods are exported.

The city of Da Nang is on the Bay of Da Nang, which is part of the South China Sea. It is Vietnam's largest port. One side of the city is sheltered from harsh weather by the Annamese Cordillera. But the other side is battered by typhoons every year.

Like other large cities in Vietnam, Da Nang is an industrial center. The city mainly produces **textiles**. The city is famous for its fireworks contest held once a year. People come from all over the world for it!

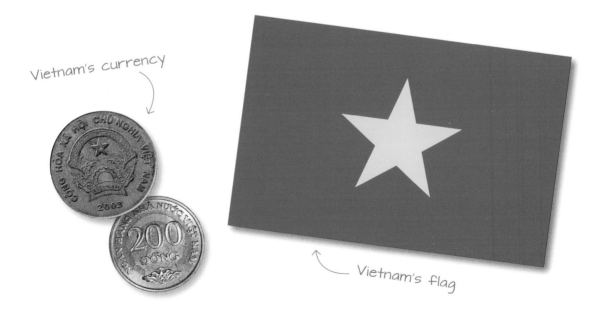

Vietnam's currency

Vietnam's flag

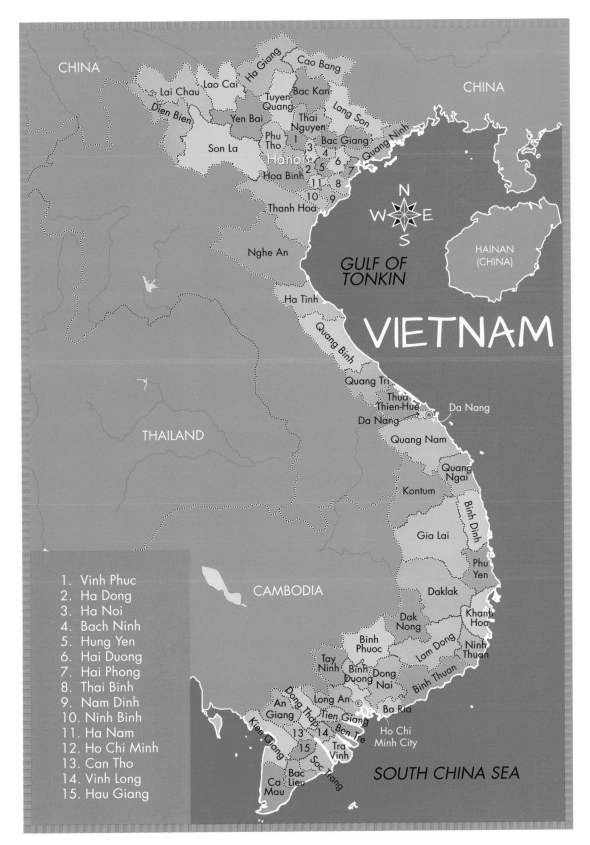

CHINA

CHINA

Ha Giang   Cao Bang

Lao Cai

Lai Chau

Dien Bien   Yen Bai   Bac Kan

Tuyen
Quang   Lang Son

Thai
Nguyen   Quang Ninh

Son La   Phu
Tho   1   Bac Giang

3   4   6   Hanoi   2   5   7

Hoa Binh   11   8

10   9

Thanh Hoa

Nghe An

GULF OF
TONKIN

HAINAN
(CHINA)

Ha Tinh

Quang Binh

VIETNAM

Quang Tri

Thua
Thien-Hue   Da Nang

Da Nang

THAILAND   Quang Nam

Quang
Ngai

Kontum

Binh Dinh

Gia Lai

Phu
Yen

Daklak

Dak
Nong   Khanh
Hoa

CAMBODIA   Binh
Phuoc   Lam Dong   Ninh
Thuan

Tay
Ninh   Binh
Duong   Dong
Nai   Binh Thuan

An
Giang   Dong Thap   Long An

Kien Giang   Tien Giang   Ben Tre   Ba Ria

13   14   Ho Chi
Minh City

15   Tra
Vinh

Soc Trang

Bac
Lieu

Ca
Mau

SOUTH CHINA SEA

1. Vinh Phuc
2. Ha Dong
3. Ha Noi
4. Bach Ninh
5. Hung Yen
6. Hai Duong
7. Hai Phong
8. Thai Binh
9. Nam Dinh
10. Ninh Binh
11. Ha Nam
12. Ho Chi Minh
13. Can Tho
14. Vinh Long
15. Hau Giang

GLOBAL CONNECTIONS

Though Vietnam is in Asia, some of its culture is French. France ruled Vietnam from 1865 to 1945. During this time, Vietnam was called French Indochina. It underwent many changes that brought in French culture.

The French set up their government in Hanoi. They built offices, government buildings, and an opera house. Many of the buildings look as though they came from Paris, France. They are made of brick and have iron gates and grand staircases.

Vietnamese writing also changed under the French. For centuries, it had used Chinese characters. The French made *Quoc-ngu* the official writing system in 1910. Instead of characters, *Quoc-ngu* uses Roman letters, just like French and English. Today this is the official writing system in Vietnam.

The French and other **missionaries** from Europe brought Christianity to Vietnam. They built Christian churches and cathedrals. Today about 9 million Vietnamese are Christians. Most practice their faith as Catholics.

CHAPTER 4

PEOPLE AND CULTURES

Vietnam has many different groups of people. There are 54 **ethnic** groups in the country. Each group has its beliefs and customs. The largest group is the Kinh. It makes up 86 percent of Vietnam's population. Kinh speak Vietnamese. Other ethnic groups speak different languages.

Vietnamese children play in the mountains while their parents tend to rice crops nearby.

Most Vietnamese people follow one of four religions. They are Buddhism, Confucianism, Taoism, and Christianity. Some people also follow ancient traditions. They worship **ancestors** and spirits.

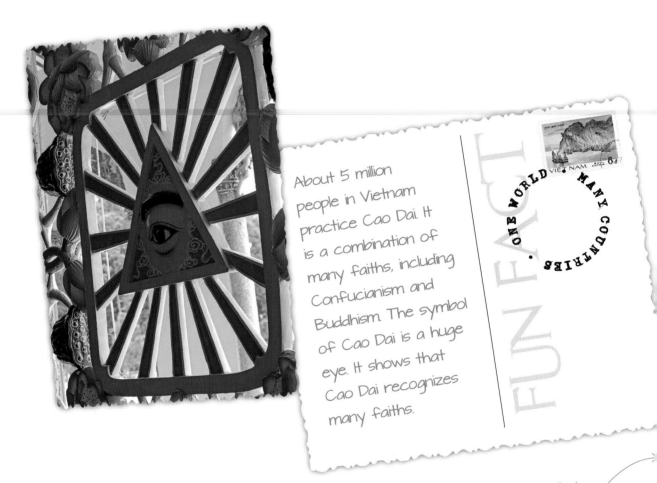

About 5 million people in Vietnam practice Cao Dai. It is a combination of many faiths, including Confucianism and Buddhism. The symbol of Cao Dai is a huge eye. It shows that Cao Dai recognizes many faiths.

FUN FACT • ONE WORLD • MANY COUNTRIES •

VIET NAM

A woman holds flower-shaped lanterns to celebrate Buddha's birthday at the Tran Quoc temple in Hanoi. Buddha was a man from India who founded the religion of Buddhism.

Music is an important part of celebrations in Vietnam. Musicians play instruments that were invented in Vietnam. One of them is the *dan bau*. It has one long string pulled tightly over a box. The musician plucks it. Musicians also use gongs and drums.

The most important celebration in Vietnam is *Tet*. It is the **lunar** New Year. To prepare for *Tet*, people repay loans. They clean their ancestors' graves. They also decorate their homes with peach blossoms and small kumquat trees.

Tet lasts for three days in late January and early February. During *Tet*, people spend time with their families. They burn **incense**. They believe the smoke rises to heaven and invites their ancestors to celebrate with them.

Another festival centers on elephants. The Elephant Racing Festival takes place every year. In one event, ten elephants race a short distance. The elephants also have a swimming match.

Vendors bring kumquat trees and flowers to sell at an open air market in Hanoi. These items are popular for decorating homes during *Tet*.

CHAPTER 5

DAILY LIFE

Going to school is part of daily life for most children in Vietnam. These students must cross a narrow river bridge on their walk to school each day.

Daily life in Vietnam's farmland begins early. People rise with the sun so they can work before it gets too hot. Men and women work together in the fields. During the heat of the afternoon, they take a break inside. They return to their work in the evening when the air is cooler.

Vietnamese children on farms often help their parents with daily chores.

The pace of life on farms is slow. Much of the work has not changed in the last century. People use animals, such as water buffalo, to work the land. The planting and harvesting is done by hand. People carry buckets of water in woven baskets to water their crops.

Life in the city has a much faster pace. It is common for workers to travel to and from work on small motorbikes. Many people work in offices or factories. They can easily visit museums, temples, and restaurants.

Women wearing *ao dai* and men in formal dress cross a monkey bridge on the way to a *Tet* festival.

Homes in Vietnam differ depending on their location. Along the Mekong River and Red River, many homes are built on stilts. This keeps them from flooding when the rivers rise. When the rivers are low, people can get into their homes using ladders. When rivers are high, they can take a boat.

Other homes float along the river. These homes have **pontoons** or empty oil drums beneath them. This allows the homes to float. Floating houses are not anchored to land. They can drift in the river.

Floating homes and stilt homes have monkey bridges. These small structures allow people to go from their homes to the shore. The bridges are made of a single bamboo log with a small handrail. Monkey bridges have been used for hundreds of years.

Vietnam's national dish is called *pho*. It is a soup with noodles, beef, and green onions. Fresh seafood and fish are

Sometimes people tie their homes together. This forms an entire village of floating homes.

commonly eaten. Many of Vietnam's dishes are served with rice. They are often seasoned with fresh herbs, such as mint, basil, and cilantro. People in Vietnam eat their meals with chopsticks.

Clothing in Vietnam is similar to that worn in the United States. Sometimes people choose to wear traditional clothing. The traditional Vietnamese clothing is called an *ao dai*. It is a long, flowing tunic worn over a pair of pants. Many years ago, men and women both wore the *ao dai*. Today only women wear it.

Life in Vietnam holds great variety. In the country, people live as they have for hundreds of years. The cities are modern, and life moves quickly. This amazing blend in Vietnam has created a country of great diversity.

Vietnamese women wearing traditional *ao dais*

DAILY LIFE FOR CHILDREN

Children in Vietnam attend school. Their mornings begin by saluting a picture of Ho Chi Minh. He was a president of Vietnam who helped shape the modern nation. Then the school day begins.

In the cities, most students wear uniforms. Most attend school from 7:00 a.m. until 1:00 p.m. When they are done with school, students work on homework or help with chores.

In the countryside, fewer children attend school. Only 10 to 15 percent of students continue school past third grade. Instead, many children work with their parents on farms.

People who live in floating houses rarely go to shore. They can do everything from the water. They can fish for food, grow herbs and plants, and raise hens all on their floating homes. They can even shop at floating markets!

FUN FACT

ONE WORLD · MANY COUNTRIES

VIET NAM

FAST FACTS

Population: 93 million

Area: 127,881 square miles (331,210 sq km)

Capital: Hanoi

Largest Cities: Ho Chi Minh City, Hanoi, and Da Nang

Form of Government: Communist State

Language: Vietnamese

Trading Partners: China, the United States, Japan, and South Korea

Major Holidays: *Tet* (Vietnamese New Year), and Elephant Racing Festival

National Dish: *Pho* (soup with noodles, beef, and green onions)

A Vietnamese woman from the Black Hmong tribe weaves a traditional bag.

GLOSSARY

ancestors (AN-sess-turz) Ancestors are people who were part of a family long ago. In Vietnam, many people honor their ancestors.

delta (DEL-tuh) A delta is an area of land made of sand and mud near the mouth of a river. Many people live in the Mekong Delta.

economy (ih-KON-uh-me) An economy is how a country runs its industry, trade, and finance. Vietnam's economy is growing.

ethnic (ETH-nik) An ethnic group has a common language, culture, religion, or background. Vietnam has 54 ethnic groups.

exported (EK-sported) Exported goods are products that have been sold to another country. Vietnam has exported many goods.

incense (IN-sense) Incense is a material that produces a pleasant scent when burned. People burn incense as a form of prayer.

lunar (LOO-nuhr) Lunar describes something relating to the moon or its cycles. The date of *Tet* is based on the lunar calendar.

missionaries (MISH-uh-ner-ees) Missionaries are people who travel to other countries to spread a religion. Missionaries brought Christianity to Vietnam.

pontoons (pawn-TOONS) Pontoons are hollow containers that float. Pontoons are placed under houses on the Mekong River.

textiles (TEK-stiles) Textiles are woven or knit fabrics or cloths. Many Vietnamese businesses make textiles.

TO LEARN MORE

BOOKS

Garland, Sherry. *Children of the Dragon: Selected Tales from Vietnam*. Gretna, LA: Pelican Publishing Co., 2012.

Polansky, Daniel. *The Vietnam War*.
New York: Scholastic Inc., 2013.

Willis, Terri. *Vietnam*. New York: Scholastic Inc., 2013.

WEB SITES

Visit our Web site for links about Vietnam: childsworld.com/links

Note to Parents, Teachers, and Librarians: We routinely verify our Web links to make sure they are safe and active sites. So encourage your readers to check them out!

INDEX